THE BATESHWAR DIARIES

GALLERIES OF TEMPLES

K BASU

ISBN 979-888521979-2

To Viewers and Readers

Contents

Gallery-I

Scenery view of Bateshwar Fair

Gallery-II

Front View of Bateshwar Fair

Gallery-III

River Yamuna View

Gallery-IV

Bank of River View

Gallery-V

River Street View

Gallery-VI

Temple View

Gallery-VII

Temple View

Gallery-VIII

Temples View

Gallery-IX

Temple View

Gallery-X

Temple View

Gallery-XI

Lord Shiva Temple

Gallery-XII

Temple View

Gallery-XIII

Temple view

Gallery-XIV

Enter Caption

Gallery-XV

FORT VIEW-I

FORT VIEW-II

FORT VIEW-III

FORT STREET

About Bateshwar

Bateshwar

Bateshwar is a village in Agra District, on the banks of the river Yamuna in the northern state of Uttar Pradesh, India. Bateshwar is in between Agra and Etawah and is 8 km from Bah. It is an important spiritual and cultural centre for Hindus and Jains. It is known for the 101 Shiv Temple Complex. An annual religious and animal fair is also organised in the village ground area.

This temple complex was built by the Bhadawar dynasty Rajput king Badan Singh Bhadawar. The name Bateshwar is derived from the main Bateshwarnath Temple dedicated to Lord Shiva (Bateshwarnath Mahadev). As per legends, here under a marvelous Banyan tree (Bat in Sanskrit), lord Shiva took rest for some time under that tree which is still standing at that place, the place hence came to be known as Bateshwar (i.e. Bat ishwar or

The banyan lord).

Since ages Bateshwar remained a renowned religious centre both for Hindu and Jain communities. In the epic Mahabharat Bateshwar is supposed to be referred as Shouripur a city of king Suresaine. It is known for 101 Shiv Temples built by Raja Badan Singh Bhadauria on a dam on the banks of Yamuna. Shaouripur, near Bateshwar, which is the birthplace of the 22nd Tirthankar of Jain faith, Lord Neminath. Each year the region hosts a cattle fair in October and November. The commercial livestock event is also of significance to Hindus, who make pilgrimage to the river Yamuna in honor of Shiva.

Bateshwar has long been celebrated for its annual fair, believed to have been a fixture since time immemorial given the significance of Shoripur/ Bateshwar in Hindu texts. Although the origins of this ancient fair are religious, and of immense importance in the Hindu religious calendar, the fair is also of great commercial value and is renowned as the 2nd largest animal fair in the country (Sonepur in Bihar being the largest).

This teerth is the birthplace of 22nd Teerthankar of Jainism, Bhagwan Shri Neminath. Following are the temples present in the area:

Baruva Matha: It is the most ancient temple of Shouripur, which is constructed on a platform. The quite magnificent Black stone's Kayotsarga idol of principal deity Bhagwan Neminath was reverenced in 1953. This idol is 8 feet high. There is a spire made of stone above the idol and behind idol there is an artistic halo is present carved in stone. On the feet base (Charan Peeth) the two lions are constructed facing each other and in between these two there is an image of Conch shell. In Yadav Jains, there is a tradition of lighting of 'Diya' on Kartik Shukla 14 here whenever there is death of any Yadav Jain takes place. Among Vaishnav Yadav Vanshi's this 'Diya' is lighted in Bateshwar on waters of Yamuna River.

Shankha Dhwaj Mandir: This temple is constructed on the second story. There are 4 altars present in the sanctum of this temple. In central altar idol of principal deity Bhagwan Neminath are installed. There are two idols of 11th – 12th century installed in this temple and the idols of Bhagwan Parshvanath, Bhagwan Chandraprabhu & Bhagwan Vimalnath reverenced are collectively installed in the second altar of this temple. Many other artistic ancient idols are also installed here.

Panch Mathi: On the left hand side of Shankha Dhwaj Mandir the ancient Tonks & spires (umbrellas) are constructed in one ground which is surrounded by walls from all sides. This place is called as Panch Mathi. The foot images of Muni 'Yama' & Muni 'Dhanya' are installed here.

Bateshwar Temple:

It is an ancient temple complex and an important spiritual and cultural centre for Hindus, is located at a distance of 70 Km from the city of Taj , Agra. The place is named after the presiding deity of the region BATESHWAR MAHADEV (another name of Lord Shiva). The temple complex consists of more than 100 temples dedicated to lord Shiva. The temples are all lined along the crescent shaped curve of the river-front and several have ghats (steps) leading down to the water. Said to be the birthplace of Lord Krishna's mother, Bateshwar is associated with numerous myths and legends. Several ancient scriptures refer to it as Surajpur in honour of its founder Raja Suraj Sen, Lord Krishna's grandfather.

Bateshwar is an important part of the Hindu pilgrimage circuit and is referred to as the 'son of the Dhams' – it must be visited once after all four Dhams considered sacred by Hindus (Badrinath in the North, Rameshwaram in the South, Dwarka in the West and Jagannath Puri in the east) have been visited.

Bateshwar Fair:

Every year a large cattle fair is held at Bateshwar (the exact dates depends on the lunar calendar and vary each year). It coincides with the most auspicious period for praying at Bateshwar and is an important fixture for saints, Sadhus, tradesmen and villagers alike. The fair attracts large numbers of Camels, Horses, oxen, elephants , goats, and other cattle, as well as a multitude of tradesmen selling everything from traditional cooking utensils and spices to locally made furniture, handicrafts and cosmetics. The fair provides a colorful, vibrant and entirely authentic glimpse of rural Indian life. Bateshwar fair is one of the largest fairs in Northern India. It stands similar in style and magnitude as compared to the Pushkar Fair in Rajasthan. This fair usually starts few days prior to DEEPAWALI (a festival of lights) for a period of almost three weeks. The first week has the animal fair starting with cattle followed by the camels and horses and ending with the donkeys and goats. And in the last week the village fair starts with a multitude of shops and fair ground rides and other attractions as well as special ceremonies in the temples.

LOCATION:

From New Delhi:

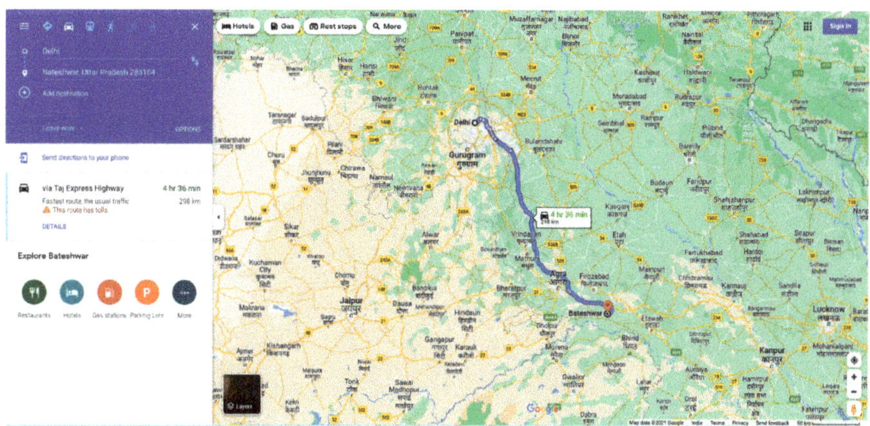

Map

From Agra:

Bateshwar is connected by road and rail. The Agra – Bah Road passes through this town and has a major impact on the development. Bateshwar Halt railway station is a small halt station. Bandra Terminus – Ghazipur City Weekly Express and Agra Cantt. – Mainpuri DEMU (via Etawah) connects the town with Mumbai, Agra, Ghazipur, Mainpuri and Etawah.Saifai Airstrip is nearest airstrip for private airplanes, Agra Airport and Gwalior Airport are two nearest domestic airports with regular scheduled flights.